Bitcoin Guide For Beginners:

Bitcoin Trading and Mining Made Easy

By

Dale Blake

Table of Contents

Introduction 5
Chapter 1. Bitcoin Basics 6
Chapter 2. Exchanges/Online Wallets................................ 14
Chapter 3. Bitcoin Facts and Myths 18
Chapter 4. Getting and Selling Bitcoins 22
Chapter 5. Bitcoin History and Criticism 25
Conclusion... 29
Thank You Page 30

Bitcoin Guide For Beginners: Bitcoin Trading and Mining Made Easy

By Dale Blake

© Copyright 2014 A Dale Blake

Reproduction or translation of any part of this work beyond that permitted by section 107 or 108 of the 1976 United States Copyright Act without permission of the copyright owner is unlawful. Requests for permission or further information should be addressed to the author.

This publication is designed to provide accurate and authoritative information in regard to the subject matter covered. This work is sold with the understanding that the publisher is not engaged in rendering legal, accounting, or other professional services. If legal advice or other expert assistance is required, the services of a competent professional person should be sought.

First Published, 2014

Printed in the United States of America

Introduction

Not many of us are familiar with the bitcoins. In this book, you will learn about some basics of bitcoins and their use. A brief overview of their merits and demerits is presented plus a comparison with the conventional currency systems and regulations. You will discover the reaction of existing governments and the banking systems to this emerging digital currency.

Bitcoin is a virtual, digital currency just like conventional currency but not printed. This model of currency is making its headway in the internet market because of ease and least regulations. While exchanging, you are not charged any fees as it is done in case of regular currencies. It can be said as a product of new globalized world in the form of single currency beyond the limitations imposed by the regional governments. It is a unique idea that will obviously inspire the whole world in the coming future.

Chapter 1. Bitcoin Basics

Bitcoin is a mode of imbursement that is online and supported by software. It saves imbursement records as public logs, and it has its own unit of accounting imbursements. The unit of measurement of imbursements is referred to as 'bitcoin'. However, the status of this kind of online currency is generally disputed and certain media groups do not recognize it as a standard currency.

The Use of Bitcoins

Bitcoins are offered as a reward for the processing of work. A user has to offer his computing power for the verification and recording imbursements in the public ledger. Such an activity is referred to as mining. Another way to obtain bitcoins is to exchange the money, products or services. This method is used other than the mining. You can use various devices for this purpose such as computer, laptop or any special purpose designed device. Here the users can electronically transfer their bitcoins for an on choice transaction fee.

Bitcoins Wallet and Account

For obtaining and processing the bitcoins, first you should have a bitcoin wallet. One must know that bitcoin is an internet-based currency, so one needs to have a place such as bitcoin wallet to save his bitcoins. Its software are available at the internet. After downloading the software, one has to proceed to download the block chain. This will lead to the client integration or registration. Once up-to-date, you should click new to obtain your wallet address. It comprises of a peculiar sequence of number and letters. You should make it sure that you have a copy of the wallet. Now you should make a data file on the pan drive; print its copy; and finally keep it safe. Different demos are available on how you should create a safe wallet, for your help. If your computer crashes for any reason, you can lose your copy of the wallet. This way may lose all of your record, so you must have all the data in your backup devices. In such a case, your bitcoins will not go to other people but they will disappear- just as burning cash.

Joining a Pool

Until now, you have a wallet and a client, so should you proceed to activate it. If you actually want to have a bitcoin, you should join a pool. It is a group where integration of computing power is done to earn more bitcoins. The underlying reason you should opt for a group is bitcoins are usually awarded in blocks such as 50 at one time. You have to be otherwise very luck to earn the bitcoins. You are given small and easy algorithms in a pool to solve. Working together will make you more likely to solve bigger and complex algorithms. This way you can earn bitcoins that are dispersed throughout the pool. It depends on your contribution. Consistency is a major factor for the higher bitcoin earning. Fragmented working does not helps a lot.

Bitcoins and Central Banks

Bitcoin can also be used to obtain things through the electronic buying. In such context, it is like a dollar or a yen that is traded digitally. Nevertheless, bitcoins are distinct, having their own peculiar characteristics. They are not controlled and regulated by a single institution as in the case of conventional currencies. Now this case has its own merits and demerits. It means that large bank will not scrutinize your money, so there is a comfort of avoiding regular long processes verifications etc. Bitcoins are not even like a print money. The banks make the matters difficult for the people because of their strict policies, new regulations and unaccountability to the people. Moreover, under the pressure of the government, and to cover up the national debts, they have to print more money thus devaluing it. But, in case of the bitcoins, the matter is other way round. They are created digitally having their own peculiar imbursement network. Bitcoins has some limitations as well. The miners cannot create more than 21 million bitcoins.

Bitcoins and Gold

The bitcoins are divided into smaller divisions where the smallest unit is Satoshi- one hundred millionth of a bitcoin. Satoshi is named after its creator. On the other side, the conventional currency is based on the gold or silver. Hypothetically, if you give a dollar to a bank you get some gold against it. However, bitcoin is based on mathematics but not on gold. All around the world the people are using software programs to produce bitcoins. The mathematical formula can easily be accessed, so it ensures transparency. Whereas, the software is an open source, anyone can use it.

Features of Bitcoins

Several important feature so bitcoins makes it unique and different from the usual fiat currencies. As already mentioned, the bitcoin network is not monitored and regulated by any single authority. Each machine that processes bitcoins is an eternal part of the whole network, where all the machines are working together. In theory, one central authority so cannot tinker with the money policy which often causes the meltdowns. It cannot make abrupt decisions such as taking people money back as it was done by the central bank of Cyprus in 2013. Furthermore, if any part of network gets offline for some reason, the whole system still keeps on going.

Easy Setup

Conventional banks make you jump through hoops simply to open a bank account. Setting up merchant accounts for imbursement is another tiring task, beset by bureaucracy. Nevertheless, one can set up a bitcoin address in seconds; no questions are asked; and no fees payable.

Multiple Bitcoin Addresses

The users can have multiple bitcoin addresses, which are not linked to names, addresses, or other personal information.

Transparency

Bitcoin stores details of every single transaction that ever happened in the network in a huge version of a general ledger. The ledger is called as the block chain. The block chain tells you everything. If you have a widely used bitcoin address, it will be possible for anyone to tell how many bitcoins are stored at that address. They just do not know whose bitcoins are these. There are measures that people can take to make their activities confidential on the bitcoin system, such as avoiding the same bitcoin addresses repeatedly, and transferring lots of bitcoin to a single address.

No fees

Your bank may charge you a £10 fee for worldwide transfers- bitcoin does not.

Quick Transaction

You can send money anywhere in minutes later, as soon as the bitcoin network processes the imbursement.

Irreversible Transaction

Once bitcoins are transferred, this transaction cannot be reversed unless the recipient does it.

Getting Bitcoins

You can get bitcoins either from exchanges or even directly from other people who are selling them. The payment can be made by hard cash, credit/debit cards, wire transfers, or even by using other crypto currencies.

Surprisingly, it is still not easy to get bitcoins with your credit card or PayPal. This is because such transactions can be reversed with a single phone call to helpline of the company. Since it is hard to prove any goods changed hands in a transfer of bitcoins, exchanges avoid this imbursement method and so do most private sellers.

However, the options have recently expanded for consumers in many countries. In the United States, Coinbase, Circle, Trucoin and coin.mx now offer purchasing. Bittylicious and CoinCorner also offer this service in the United Kingdom, which accepts 3D Secure-enabled cards on the Visa and MasterCard networks. You can use a card to get $20-worth at Tinkercoin. Under banked consumers in the United States can turn to expresscoin that was recently launched to serve this market, accepting money orders, personal checks and wire transfers.

Chapter 2. Exchanges/Online Wallets

The range of choices are now expanding making headway. Now, new trades are venturing online to cater to the new markets. Some employ trades between the paper sanction currencies and various digital currencies while some employ simple wallet services. These simpler wallet services are a more limited range of trading options. Many of these can store digital or fiat currency just like the conventional banks.

If you want to engage yourselves into some kind of regular trading, exchanges are the best option. Here you do not depend upon lengthy bureaucratic procedure and have a secrecy. Such processes usually require the proofs of you identity and other personal details. This kind of law is prevalent in most countries and no regulated exchange can get around it.

Warnings about Exchanges, Banks and Wallets

However, the lack of proof of the identity requirements have also many drawbacks. There is no insurance of the accounts because these are not regulated. You may face hacking or other issues.

Moreover, bitcoins have not legal standing as the currency has in the world. On the other side, the authorities do not have much awareness about bitcoins and legal instruments available, so theft cannot be traced back and reported. Some well-reputed companies have provided some refunds and securities but still they are not obliged to do so. Furthermore, if any theft occurs from your personal wallet due to a security or password lapse, then you are left with no guaranteed ways to get back your funds.

Banks see the digital currency model as a threat to their business, so they do not offer cooperation and services in this field. Even knowing anything about the accountholder dealing in bitcoins, they close the account without any explanation. Mining the bitcoins with your PC and powerful graphics card was even not possible earlier. But the time and the increasing popularity of this online currency have brought many powerful device, mining specific in the market, thereby increasing the difficulty and energy required to mine worthwhile amounts of bitcoin. Furthermore, the bitcoins left for mining diminishes very sharply with time. It simply means that to mine as an individual is not as cost effective as it was a couple of months ago. Unluckily, many have paid more for the hardware and other auxiliaries than they earned.

Mining has become the domain of guilds- a large mining group. The companies have ventured specifically for mining. You can get shares in such as guild. However, mining is not like a hobby, a tough job. Other option is 'cloud mining'. Here one can mine bitcoins with no need to invest in expensive and fast-speed equipment. A person has to pay to use company's data centers to mine on its behalf.

The investment trust is another way e.g Bitcoin Investment Trust (BIT). If you are not willing to store large quantity of bitcoins then you can use this idea. This trust invests in bitcoins exclusively. It uses a protocol to store them safely on behalf of its shareholders. Until now, the fund is exclusively for serious investors.

Bitcoins ATMs

The recent development in the field of bitcoins are the ATMs. These are spilling all over the world very rapidly. There are many vendors dealing in these ATMs such as

Robcoin, Lasammu, CoinOutler and Bitaccess. Just like a face-to-face exchange, here in these ATMs, you have to insert your cash. Moreover, you have to scan your mobile wallet that contains a QR code. In other case, you can also receive a paper receipt with written codes required to load the bitcoins in your wallet.

As the beginners usually assume, bitcoin is not an easy way-out. However, there is also good news there increasing options that have broadened the horizons. For the entrepreneurs, every day there are plethora of incentives to invent more convenient ways. Even internet access or a wallet are not the only options. There are also some more ideas such as bitcoin gift cards, physical bitcoins, and value-stored cards.

Chapter 3. Bitcoin Facts and Myths

There are many myths and bad stories attached with bitcoins. With their growing popularity, everyone wanted to become a millionaire. In doing so, because of no identities involved, many black markets emerged in trading using bitcoins. A popular example is notorious black market, known to many as the Silk Road. The authorities seized million of dollars worth bitcoins. We also saw efforts to unveil the identity of its inventor Satoshi Nakamoto. Even we listened to the experts involved in debate about the future of bitcoins. There were of people who followed blindly, but there are a few who took it seriously and cautiously.

Now bitcoin is emerging in its stable and mature phase. It is getting more robust and legitimate while its protagonists are pushing for its adoption. The efforts are being made to turn bitcoin into a currency rather than an asset or a financial lark and make the most of its unique capabilities. The ease, quickness and simplicity are the bigger reasons of the increasing popularity of bitcoins in the world. However, still it is lagging behind the conventional currency due to various issues and lesser confidence of market on it.

Bitcoin is at its core a cryptographic protocol, so it is also referred to as a 'crypto-currency.' This protocol generates unique pieces of digital property. These can be transferred from one person to another. The protocol also prevents double spending a Bitcoin, meaning you cannot spend the same Bitcoin more than one time.

Bitcoins are generated by using a computer program. It solves the complex math problems in a process called mining. Each Bitcoin is defined by a public address and a private key. These are long strings of numbers and letters giving each a particular identity. It means that Bitcoin is not only a token of value but also a method for transferring that value.

In addition to having a unique digital fingerprint, bitcoins are identified by their position in a public ledger. Getting a bitcoins is like getting a space in the blockchain. This blockchain records purchase permanently and publicly.

Getting a Bitcoin can be thought of as getting a spot in the blockchain that records your purchase publicly and permanently. The blockchain is maintained by a distributed network of computers all around the world.

A single entity does not control it. Transactions occur digitally from among the people, without intermediaries such as banks or special clearinghouses. The network of public bitcoin is the official record holder for all of these transactions.

The direct approach is generally used that significantly reduces the payment of fees a condition attached with transferring traditional money. This makes bitcoin system much easier and quick to transfer the money all across the world. Bitcoin gives an increase in efficiency comparable to banking transactions and to the efficiency of email versus physical email. The people primarily get and sell bitcoins through online exchanges network. The private keys and public address are both required to trade, sell, and spend bitcoins.

The identities of traders are kept hidden from each other because the transactions are made using the public keys. The transactions have to be recorded publicly. Bitcoins are commonly known to be unanimous but pseudonymous word can be referred to more appropriately. Unfortunately, bitcoins are associated with illicit activities because tracing back the transactions is not possible. So it is biggest flaw in bitcoins. For instance, the case of selling and buying g drugs on the defunct Silk Road market is an example.

As it is in the case of paper money, bitcoins can also be saved but in the digital wallet. Actually, this wallet stores the public and private keys used to identify the bitcoins and to make the transaction. These wallets can be secured in the cloud environment on internet or on your computer and even they can take some kind of physical form as well. Here, you should know that if your keys are lost, you can no longer access your bitcoins. Either you can use your bitcoins to purchase items from the online merchants and all those organizations that accept it or they can be cashed in any exchange. You can also involve any broker.

Chapter 4. Getting and Selling Bitcoins

You know that a government decides how many notes to be printed and when to be printed. However, the case with bitcoins is other way around. They do not depend on the state banks, but are created through mining. Mining is also called as hashing. It is a process of solving complex math problems using those computers which run bitcoin software. Here, for this, much higher computing speed is required than usually available. Hence, the people use specialized king of bitcoin machine, or they have to form a network of machines for integration of the whole process. If, by using your, program you solve one problem, one block is created and this reward process keeps going on.

These are the cryptographic puzzles, which become increasingly harder to solve as more bitcoins gets into the circulation. In addition, rather than increasing as normally in other cases occur, the reward decreases by half. Here, as already discussed the maximum limit is 21 million. No sooner it is achieved than the process stops immediately. You must know that even a single bitcoin worth a lot.

The blocks, created by mining, produce the transaction record of the bitcoin. Every block contains in it a hash of the previous block, which creates a transaction. The blockchain records all transactions in chronological order. A new block is added to the blockchain- an average of once every ten minutes. It is distributed across all the mining computers, rather than being maintained by a central body.

How do you get or sell Bitcoins?

Fortunately, you not have do indulge and confuse yourselves in the nuances of letters such as hashes and nodes. Moreover, you not need to be confused in the blockchains. The exchanges are also a good option but not an obligation. You just need to have a bitcoin wallet to trade through an exchange. There are many reputed exchanges such as Mt. Gox, Bitcoin.de and Virt Ex. Fixed rate exchanges are also there such as Coinbase.

Do not forget, you must be very careful about where you place your trust and your money: bitcoin exchanges are not regulated. Although, it appeals many, it makes swindling easier. Once you are settled with a broker or an exchange, you have to link you bank account. For this, you need to have an account with a user name and a password. Every exchange has its own peculiar mythologies like Coinbase asks for your phone number. Some exchange even deal in real world money- exchanging your bitcoins with print currency. Sometimes there is a time-delay for the beginners for the processing of orders.

Whenever, you want to sell your bitcoins, assure first that you have bitcoins there. Now all what you have to do is to click sell. Making transactions of bitcoins is thought as safer. As pointed out before, every Bitcoin has a unique, private, and long numerical identification number. By writing this key down or by storing it on a local drive, you can trade a Bitcoin just by passing that key off to other person. LocalBitcoins.com is a platform that connects people who are looking to get and sell locally with trading partners. There are all around the world more than 4,500 locations for the trading of bitcoins. This approach can actually be faster than going through a centralized exchange. Moreover, it offers more flexible imbursement options, such as PayPal, cash, and Western Union.

Chapter 5. Bitcoin History and Criticism

A Brief Overview of History

The idea of bitcoins was first presented by Satoshi Nakamoto in his research paper in 2008. Hal Finney- a cryptographer- was the first man who supported and adopted bitcoins. The day the software was released, he bought it and received 10 bitcoins from Nakamoto. Since then, this currency system witnessed very rapid growth. Many mainstream websites such as Wordpress, Atomic Mail, Tigerdirect began its use. With time, many non-profit, private organization began accepting the donations in bitcoins. Electronic frontier Foundation was the first to venture into this arena. But unfortunately, the use of bitcoins entered in the black market which maligned its image. This occurred when the US homeland Security department seized Mt. Gox Exchange. Later, stringent measures was also taken by the Chinese government.

Vancouver, Canada has the honor of having the first ever bitcoin ATM installed in 2013. Bitcoins witnessed such a rapid boom that within months total market capitalization of bitcoins swelled from 12 million to $10 billion.

Criticism

Bitcoin has seen growth as a form of imbursement for products and services. The online traders have a reason to accept the digital currency because charges are less than the 2–3%, which are normally imposed by credit card processing companies. Nevertheless, the European banking authority has shown reservations regarding the security of the transaction processed through bitcoins. In these transactions, unlike credit cards, the fees are paid by the purchaser not by the vendor. Bitcoins can be stolen; charge-backs are difficult. As of July 2013, the commercial use of bitcoin was low as compared to its use by opportunists, which has contributed to price instability.

The use of bitcoins for the unlawful activities is under severe criticism. Bitcoins are sometimes used to purchase corrupt items, including child pornography, credit card details, and drugs. They are seized by authorities when such sites are shut down. The United States is more bitcoin-friendly than that of some other governments. In China, getting bitcoin with Yuan is subject to limitations, and bitcoin exchanges are not allowed to hold bank accounts.

Currency or a Protocol

There is an unending debate whether bitcoins is a currency or a payment protocol. Its definition is vague which ignited this debate. However, despite such a confusion, it is generally referred to as a digital currency or a virtual currency. Money is generally defined as a store of value, an exchange medium and an accounting unit mutually agreed. According to criteria, bitcoins are a medium of exchange because the traders accept it for the barter.

Volatility

Bitcoins are highly volatile that limits the ability of bitcoins to act as a stable store. To understand this issue, consider that still prices are stated in the local currency and bitcoins are used for the transactions. This issue illuminated the problem of volatility. You cannot price you product as 100 bitcoins or 20 bitcoins. Bitcoins are being arbitrarily classified by the various departments because of lack of clarity. The bank of china does not accept it as a currency while European central banks regards it a virtual currency.

It is reported that bitcoins are seven times more volatile than gold and eighteen times greater than the US dollar. This estimation speaks volumes of the extent of the issue of volatility. The prices of bitcoins are ever changing rapidly- appreciating and depreciating frequently. For instance, it reached equivalent to $266 at one instance and $50 at other instance. However, this volatility is not a big concern in black economy markets such as gambling, and drugs. Moreover, it is lesser concern in the international remittances.

Conclusion

Hence, bitcoin can be the next future currency of the world because of diminishing importance of regular currency at one side and increasing relevance of quick and speedy means, such as bitcoins, on the other side. We have already seen how ATMs and online services have partly replaced the existing systems of transactions- trading and banking. Similarly, this newly system, though less popular yet, will soon begin the onslaught of conventional systems.

This online currency system is facing tough resistance from the monopolization and manipulations of status quo banks and exchanges. Despite this resistance, its popularity is on swift rise. The reason is its ease, quickness and simplicity. In this situation, the awareness of this bitcoin currency is far more relevant and urgent. This book is a humble attempt to introduce you about bitcoins in a comprehensive and simple manner.

Thank You Page

I want to personally thank you for reading my book. I hope you found information in this book useful and I would be very grateful if you could leave your honest review about this book. I certainly want to thank you in advance for doing this.

www.ingramcontent.com/pod-product-compliance
Lightning Source LLC
LaVergne TN
LVHW021746060526
838200LV00052B/3503